HEROES AND WARRIORS

CUCHULAINN

HOUND OF ULSTER

BOB STEWART
Plates by JAMES FIELD

Firebird Books

First published in the UK 1988 by Firebird Books

Copyright © 1988 Firebird Books Ltd, P.O. Box 327, Poole, Dorset BH15 2RG
Text copyright © 1988 R.J. Stewart

Distributed in the United States by
Sterling Publishing Co, Inc.
2 Park Avenue, New York, NY 10016

Distributed in Australia by
Capricorn Link (Australia) Pty Ltd
P.O. Box 665, Lane Cove, NSW 2066

British Library Cataloguing in Publication Data

Stewart, Bob
   Cuchulainn : Hound of Ulster.——(Heroes and warriors series).
   1. Cuchulainn (Legendary character) 2. Legends, Irish
   I. Title II. Series
   398′.352   GR153.5

ISBN 1 85314 003 1

Series editor Stuart Booth
Designed by Kathryn S.A. Booth
Typeset by Colset Private Limited, Singapore
Colour separation by Kingfisher Facsimile
Colour printed by Butler and Tanner, Frome and London
Printed in Great Britain by Richard Clay Ltd, Chichester, Sussex

CUCHULAINN

HOUND OF ULSTER

THE IRELAND OF CUCHULAINN

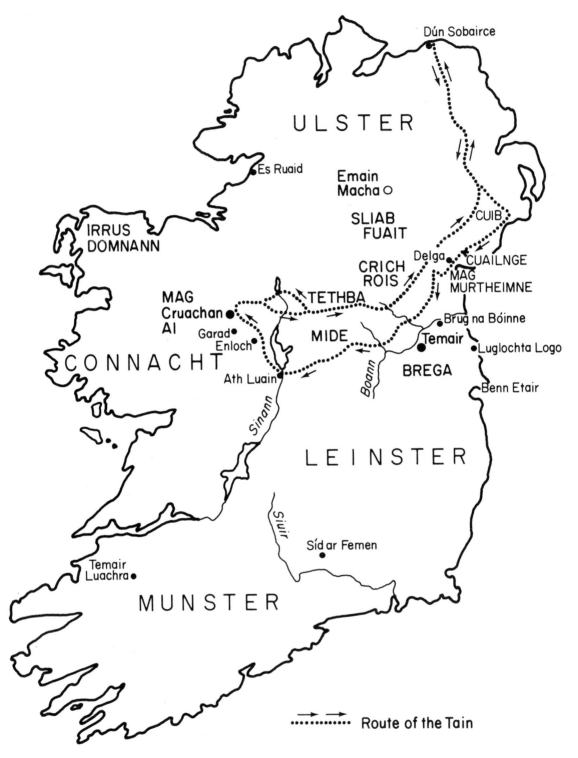

ULSTER

Dún Sobairce

Es Ruaid

Emain Macha ○

SLIAB FUAIT

IRRUS DOMNANN

CRICH ROIS

CUIB

Delga

CUAILNGE

MAG MURTHEIMNE

MAG Cruachan AI

TETHBA

Brug na Bóinne

Garad ● Enloch ●

MIDE

Temair

Luglochta Logo

CONNACHT

Ath Luain

BREGA

Benn Etair

Sinann

Boann

LEINSTER

Siuir

Síd ar Femen

Temair Luachra ●

MUNSTER

············▶ Route of the Tain

The Cuchulainn Saga

To examine Cuchulainn in depth has been the task of many great Irish language and Celtic scholars over the last century or more. In this simple retelling of those adventures are selected insights into the cultural background wherever facts can be confirmed. To look at Cuchulainn's culture, weapons, battles, and mythical or magical origins is to combine evidence from a number of sources.

First and foremost, the early Irish texts in which this great champion features are extensive and very complex. So, in looking at the basic, important themes and adventures, many of the lesser stories have to be omitted.

The Cuchulainn texts do not stand alone; they are related to a number of other Celtic legendary sources, many of which are not Irish but British. Thus we have to look at comparisons between themes in Cuchulainn and those in the legends of King Arthur as they arise in discussion of the champion and his adventures. As with the warriors of Arthur, or the ancient Greek heroes, we find the dim echoes of divinity in these legends of the origins of our hero; whoever or whatever Cuchulainn was originally, by the time the great tales and sagas had been built around the astonishing exploits of himself and his men, he was of magical and semi-divine proportions and ability.

The feats of the warriors of Ulster were indeed magical; they were able to kill hundreds of men with ease, they ate entire oxen and drank vats of alcohol; they cut the tops of hills away with their mighty swords, and boiled their bath water with their furious body heat.

The tales of Cuchulainn also consist of a rich complex of magical and pagan religious symbols, found as adventures, mysterious locations, curious taboos, and a host of other specific and often rather startling features within the structure of the epic tales. Clearly, there is far more to Cuchulainn than his superhuman strength and skill in arms. These abilities and natural gifts may be one of the main reasons why his adventures have survived. Yet underneath these heroic deeds runs a deeper and more enduring layer of high adventure, transformation and growth, and the perilous mysteries of the Otherworld or Underworld.

Finally, there is hard physical archaeological evidence that corresponds to material in the Cuchulainn texts. This includes physical locations such as the fortress of Emain Macha (now called Navan Fort), many early finds of weaponry and armour, and the most significant use of natural locations such as islands, rivers, and countries in the development of the legends.

It soon becomes clear that Cuchulainn moved not merely in a localised circuit of Ulster in Northern Ireland, but upon a broader basis to Britain in general. This ease of movement from Ireland to Scotland reveals a culture in which an overall unity – loosely defined as Celtic – seems to have existed. Such a unity is supported by the writings of classical authorities, such as Julius Caesar, who took some care to describe the religion of the Celts, certain aspects of druidism, and the fact that the culture had a type of religious unity, despite being decentralised politically or geographically. We find exactly this same picture in the Cuchulainn tales; the unity was found through religious and magical practices and beliefs, which transcended tribal boundaries; yet powerful kingdoms made war upon one another within this overall unity. This last aspects of conflict out of deep unity is a typically Celtic character-istic, and persists even today.

Origins of the Saga

The preservation of the Cuchulainn saga is as remarkable as its origins; the extended story-cycle comes from a bardic or oral tradition of great sophisti-cation. The complexity of the descriptions, the cultural ambience, and the vast body of material that corresponds to historical and archaeological or early literary parallels leaves us in no doubt that this is the product of a civilised and complex people. That the original culture was heroic, consisted of head-hunters and warriors and had a strict magical–religious foundation does not in any way debar us from calling the pagan Irish sources for Cuchulainn civilised. They had central locations, such as Emain Macha, now known as Navan Fort, a highly organised governmental structure, and extremely well defined rules of behaviour for all aspects of life.

The origins of the translated material used here are even more curious than our speculations and knowledge about pagan Celtic civilisation. They were transcribed by monks, probably from oral tradition, and preserved in monas-tic libraries. The oldest example of Cuchulainn tales is the *Book of the Dun Cow* from the monastry of Clonmacnoise. *The Book of Leinster* was tran-scribed by Finn mac Gorman, the Bishop of Kildare. When we examine the broader spectrum of preserved material, it is clear that monastic chroniclers and transcribers took great care to set out the oral tradition. This was still maintained in the days of the early Church in Britain and Ireland by bards and poets, the descendants of the same druidic caste system which plays such an important role in the adventures of Cuchulainn and the Red Branch warriors.

Curiously, the overt pagan and magical elements were not written out of the Cuchulainn material, as we might expect. The short examples quoted here might have been enlarged by a significant number of extracts which clearly demonstrate magical arts, pagan religion, and druidic lore. Those included tend to bear directly upon the skills, adventures, and doom, of

warriors; but they reveal this totally un-Christian element. There are, of course, Christian interpolations and deliberate alterations of chronology in the full body of the Cuchulainn texts. But it is clear that the Irish monks held the Hound of Ulster and his not so distant pagan world in great respect; so much so that they did not suppress or rewrite or destroy, as many other Christians have done through the centuries.

In the context of this account of the hero, literary and historical comparisons are unimportant other than to show the drama and power of the basic character and tales. The reader who wishes to go into the subject in depth will find an immense wealth of other reference material, scholarship, and speculation. The most recent detailed annotated translation is *The Tain* by Thomas Kinsella.

Bronze brooch from Emain Macha, now in the British Museum.

Weapons and Warrior Training

The weapons of Cuchulainn's culture were basically those of the early Celts, with a number of very specific and individual items unique to certain characters. In addition to the actual hardware, we may also include a number of other less usual but certainly very prominent and important weapons used in

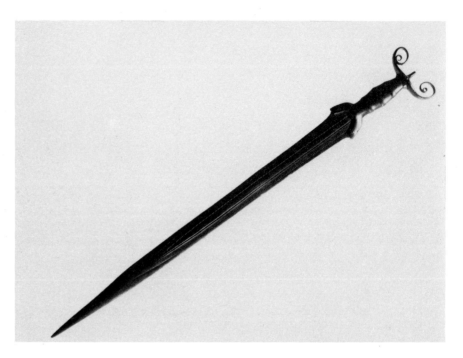

Late Bronze Age sword, now in the British Museum. This weapon is probably very close to the kind carried by Cuchulainn.

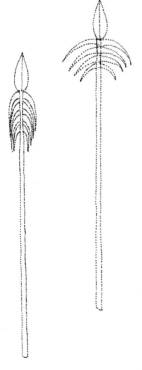

Reconstruction of the gae bulga, Cuchulainn's barbed spear which was thrown with the feet.

the various conflicts in which the Champion of Ulster was engaged. These are, of course, the magical weapons, skills, and illusions which abound through the Cuchulainn legends.

Basic weapons were the spear, sword, sling – and the shield which could be used as an offensive weapon with sharpened rims. Many of these weapons were famed in themselves.

Spears
The Gapped spear of King Conchobar.
The Venomous spear of King Conchobar.
The *Culghlas* or blue-green spear of Conall the Victorious.
The *Cual gae* or grouping of spears and swords; perhaps similar to the medieval *chevaux de frise*.

Swords
Caladcholg, the sword of Fergus Mac Roich (Roy) which stretched to the length of a rainbow; this was a sword from the *sidhe* or Otherworld.
The sword of Manannan mac Lir which left no sign of stroke or blow behind.
The *Cruaiden cadatchenn*, Cuchulainn's hereditary sword; the name means something like 'dear little hard one'.

Shields
The Bright Rim of King Conchobar.
Cuchulainn's shield of dark crimson with a pure white silver rim.
Missive or throwing shields with sharp edges, used as offensive weapons.

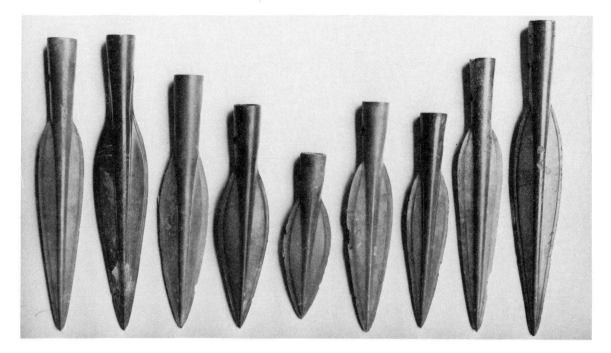

One such shield cut off the hero Sualtam's head in a mysterious accident
   leading to a magical prophecy.

The large bossed shield of Fergus Mac Roich, with fifty bosses that could each
   bear the weight of a hog, and a great central boss of red gold.

*   *   **

Body armour was worn by certain heroes, sometimes in conjunction with
chariots with scythe bearing wheels, trained war horses and special spears
such as five-pointed weapons and the *gae bulga*.

This curious and highly individual weapon was a type of harpoon with
retractable barbs, similar to a number of tearing or lodging spears and arrows
used in historical warfare. The *gae bulga* was originally given by Scathach the
warrior woman to Aoife, who Cuchulainn conquered as a test and task in
service of Scathach. Therefore, it seems that it was passed from the second
warrior woman to the Champion of Ulster at the time of her defeat. This is
significant, as an indication of the powers of fate, for it was Aoife's son (by
Cuchulainn) who was tragically slain by his father, using the *gae bulga*. It is
worth quoting in full the technique described for throwing this deadly
weapon, from the duel between Cuchulainn and Ferdiad:

Then Cuchulainn asked Laeg [his charioteer] for the *gae bulga*. The manner of the weapon
was this; it had to be set down the stream, and cast from between the toes. It made the
wound of one spear entering the body, but it had thirty barbs to open and could not be with-
drawn from the body but must be cut out . . . the servant set the spear down the stream and
Cuchulainn caught it between the toes of his foot and threw an unerring cast at
Ferdiad. . . .

9

The *gae bulga* passed through Ferdiad's firm deep apron of wrought iron, and broke the great stone as large as a mill stone (set over his lower body as a shield) into three parts. It passed through these protective coverings into his body, so that every crevice and every cavity of him was filled with its barbs.

The standard techniques and motifs of fighting included single combat (rather than multiple pitched battles), seen later to good effect in the context of the Cattle Raid of Cooley. Champion charioteers and chariots were used as fighting units and there were formalised or ritualised modes of combat and challenge. Raiding and stealing over tribal boundaries were common sources of combat.

Unusual techniques of deliberate conflict, widespread in all tales, included magical attacks such as weakening or debilitating sleep, illusions of great armies, monstrous beasts and opponents from the Otherworld. There were also the druidic techniques of satire, undeniable requests, music and poetry, and *geasa*, a system of unavoidable taboos which were often used as weapons or tactical devices to gain power or control situations.

Divine intervention, the continual and essential intervention of gods and goddesses or other supernatural beings occurs very often in the legends. Indeed most of the tales hinge upon such intervention, often through a complex chain of events, *geasa*, parentage, meetings, challenges, tests and dedications.

The Duel
The duel between the Hound of Ulster and Ferdiad provides us with another detailed and colourful description of heroic combat techniques:

'Do you remember, the throwing weapons that we used to practise with Scathach?' said Ferdiad.
    'I remember them indeed,' replied Cuchulainn.
    'Then let us use them against one another,' said Ferdiad.

The account then continues:

So they took their throwing shields in their hands, and their eight turned handled spears, and their eight little quill spears, and their eight ivory hilted swords, and their eight sharp ivory handled spears. The weapons flew back and forward between them like bees on the wing on a sunny day. Till midday they fought with these weapons. . . .

Warrior Training
During the scene described above, both champions referred to their training together under the instruction of the warrior woman Scathach. During this part of the Cuchulainn saga, we find once again some interesting detailed observations upon the traditional techniques taught to the ancient Celtic warrior:

At last, when the full lore of soldierly arts had been mastered by Cuchulainn; the apple-feat, the thunder-feat, the blade-feat, the supine-feat, the spear-feat, the rope-feat, the body-feat, the cat's-feat, the salmon-feat of a chariot chief, the throw of the staff, the whirl of a brace

Typical bronze helmet from a Celtic grave. The use of bronze for armour and weaponry appears to have persisted among Celtic tribes long after the appearance of iron.

chariot chief, the spear of the bellows (*gae bulga*), the *boi* of swiftness, the wheel-feat, the breath-feat, the *brud geme*, the hero's whoop, the blow, the counter blow, running up a lance and righting the body upon its point; the scythe chariot and the twisting around spear points . . . when he had learned all this a message came to him to return to his own land, and so he took his leave.

This list is extremely detailed, and derives from a precise tradition of combat techniques.

Cuchulainn – Man and Legend

According to Irish tradition Cuchulainn, as leader of the great hero band of Ulster, lived at the beginning of the Christian era. Indeed, his king Conchobar MacNessa, is said to have died of fury upon hearing of the death of Christ. This interesting rationalisation of early Irish history is likely to be religious propaganda, but like many traditions may have some element of truth within it. We may reasonably date a historical Cuchulainn to the first century B.C. at the very latest. As we shall soon discover, many elements of his story and his culture obviously come from a much earlier period.

It seems likely, as with many legendary heroes (such as King Arthur and the Knights of the Round Table) that a fusion of historical tradition and magical or mythical tradition surrounds Cuchulainn and the band of warriors of Ulster. In such cases, a real hero becomes part of a myth, such as that of the victorious sun. This occurs not merely because he seems to be a brightly-shining and divine person, when tales and songs are woven around him, but because such heroes and kings, even as real persons, were part of a pagan culture in which they held a semi-divine status. Cuchulainn is said to have been a son of the Gaelic sun-god; this may be myth or a poetic memory of the fact that such warriors were dedicated body and soul to the early gods and goddesses of pagan Ireland.

Lineage of Cuchulainn
On his mother's side Cuchulainn was the grandson of the Dagda, whose name simply means 'the good god'. The Dagda was a primal giant figure, one of the dimly remembered but extremely potent first deities of the Celts; humorous and scurrilous tales were told about this lusty, powerful, hungry giant. As if this grandparentage was not sufficient, Cuchulainn was also said to be the son of Lugh Long Hand, whose name means 'Light', a very direct image of the ancient Celtic sun god.

The mother of Cuchulainn was Dechtire, daughter of Maga, grand-daughter of Angus 'Son of the Young', and half-sister to King Conchobar. Thus the King and his hero were related.

Bronze scabbard from Co. Antrim, Ireland; a typical weapon from the sagas.

11

King Conchobar and his Court

King Conchobar MacNessa, blood relative and ruler of Cuchulainn held court at Emain Macha. As with so many apparently mythical sagas, there is a physical location attached to the tradition of Conchobar and his court. Near Armagh, the extensive prehistoric fortress, Navan Fort is imposing and atmospheric to this day. Archaeologists are still investigating this ancient and impressive site, which ceased to be used around 90 B.C.

From here, Conchobar ruled the kingdom of Ulster which extended southwards as far as the Boyne. It was at this location that the astonishing band of heroes assembled, under the undisputed leadership of Cuchulainn.

The relationship between Cuchulainn and his mythical or divine father and grandfather becomes all the more apparent when we study the descriptions of his nature and his physical attributes. He was small and insignificant in size, yet no one could look full upon him in his glory without blinking. The very heat of his burning body could melt snow and ice for yards around; he glowed red and when he dipped his body to bathe in the sea, the waters hissed and steamed. Perhaps the most dramatic description of Cuchulainn is his battle fury, which was the most ferocious ever known among the many Celtic heroes and warriors:

Among the clouds over his head could be seen seething pouring showers and sparks of red fire, which his savage wrath caused to mount upwards above him. His hair became tangled about his head, as if it had been branches of a red thorn bush stuffed into a strongly fenced gap. . . . Taller thicker and more rigid than the mast of a great ship was the jet of dusky blood which shot upwards out of the very centre of his scalp, to be scattered to the four cardinal points (of east, south, west, and north). From this fountain was formed a magical mist of gloom, resembling the smoky pall which drapes a royal hall, at nightfall of a winters day.

(Tain Bo Chuailgne)

Birth of Cuchulainn

Like many heroes with a curious semi-magical or divine origin, Cuchulainn had a miraculous birth. His mother Dechtire was sitting at her wedding feast, about to be married to the Ulster chieftain Sualtam. Into her cup of wine flew a mayfly, which she swallowed without noticing its presence. Soon she fell into a deep sleep in which the sun-god Lugh appeared to her as if in a dream. Lugh told her that it had been no mere mayfly that she had swallowed, but himself.

After delivering this revelation, Lugh transformed Dechtire and her fifty maidens into the shape of a beautiful flock of birds, and so they disappeared without trace. After months had passed, the warriors of Emain Macha were lured out to hunt, drawn by the appearance of a flock of birds.

Riding in their chariots until nightfall, pursuing the elusive flock, the men of Ulster suddenly realised that they had been lured to the Brugh na Boyne which was the home of the gods and goddesses of the land. Before the warriors arose a splendid hall, of a beauty and size such as they had never before seen. A tall, handsome chieftain, very richly attired, came out of the hall and welcomed them, offering them hospitality. When the warriors

entered this marvellous place, they found seated there a beautiful woman and fifty lovely maidens; upon the tables was set a feast of meat and wine such as would grace the hall of a great king.

The Court House in modern Dundalk, the town traditionally cited as the home of Cuchulainn.

The Ulster warriors rested for the night, and during their rest they heard the cry of a new born babe. In the morning, Lugh revealed his true name to them, and told them that the woman was no other than the half-sister of Conchobar, and that she had given birth to a child who was to be taken back to grow up among the warriors at the Ulster court. Thus the mother, the baby boy and maidens returned; all the heroes, Druids, poets, and lawgivers of Ulster gave the best of their skills and wisdom to the infant as instructed.

Naming of Cuchulainn

At first the baby boy was called Setanta but this was to change in that most magical manner by which heroes acquire their true names, i.e. through unusual and highly symbolic circumstances. As a child, Setanta was the

13

strongest boy in Emain Macha, champion of all sports. One day, while playing hurley single-handed against a team of the other boys, and beating them, he was summoned by King Conchobar. The king who had watched his skill and was impressed by the child's ability, commanded him to come to a feast at the house of Culann the chief blacksmith. Setanta promised to come as soon as he had finished the game.

When the Ulster champions entered the smith's hall, the king gave permission for Culann to let loose his terrible watch hound, fiercer than any hundred other dogs. But they had forgotten that the child was following them (after winning his game of hurley). When the savage hound attacked Setanta, he threw his ball into its mouth, and grabbing it by the legs, dashed out its brains against a rock.

Culann the chief smith was enraged at the loss of his guard hound, but the child promised to find him another and train it for him. He also undertook to guard the hall of the smith himself, just as the hound would have done, until a replacement was fully trained. Thus Setanta became Cuchulainn, which means 'The Hound of Culann'.

The Druid of the royal court, Cathbad, prophesied that this child's name would one day be known and spoken by every man in Ireland; which was not surprising with such a remarkable parentage and childhood promise of skill and strength.

One day, Cuchulainn overheard Cathbad giving instruction in the lore of druidism, and one of the pupils asked for what would the day be propitious. The answer was that any young man taking arms that day would gain a greater name than any other hero, but that his life would be short. Cuchulainn immediately asked King Conchobar for arms and a chariot, declaring that the Druid had predicted this to be a day for the arming of a hero.

On this first day of bearing arms, and commanding his own chariot and charioteer, the young Cuchulainn went into battle and killed three champions who had long harassed the warriors of Ulster. He brought back their heads to the hall of the King. At this time he was reputedly only seven years old.

Cuchulainn and Love

It is hardly surprising that such a miraculous youth should grow at a rate faster than that of any normal child. So it was not long before the women of Ulster paid so much attention to the young Cuchulainn that the other warriors became extremely jealous. They demanded that his youthful exploits be tamed by his taking of a wife; but he was not an easy person to please in the choice of a prospective bride. Cuchulainn swore that he would have only one maiden as his bride, Emer, the daughter of Forgal the Wily. She was the maiden in all of Ireland who had the best of the six gifts of maidenhood; chastity, wisdom, needlework, sweet speech, singing, and of course beauty. No other young woman was her equal. But when Cuchulainn went to court her, she laughed at him, saying that he was merely a boy. He swore a great oath that he would make his name known wherever the deeds of heroes were

related . . . and Emer finally promised that she would marry him if he could take her away from her warlike family.

The Isle of Skye, where young men like Cuchulainn, from Scotland and Ireland, were trained by the warrior woman Scathach.

Scathach the Warrior Woman

However, Forgal the Wily lived up to his name, and devised a plan by which he hoped to be rid of this troublesome suitor. Deliberately, he went to visit Emain Macha, pretending never to have heard of Cuchulainn. When he saw this remarkable youth win at every game, challenge, test, and feat of arms or skill, Forgal declared that such a hero should go to the island of Scathach the Warrior Woman, situated in Alba (Scotland). This curious stronghold, usually identified as the Isle of Skye (Scathach is pronounced 'Sca-hah') was difficult to reach, and even more difficult to escape from unscathed. Forgal hoped that rather than gain training in arms from the fearsome Scathach, Cuchulainn would meet his death.

The tradition of Celtic warrior women is not limited to this reference to Scathach, for women were accustomed and sometimes obliged to bear arms as late as the sixth century. That the great heroes should go for arms training to a warrior woman living on an isolated island is not so unusual when we

15

remember that the most terrible and warlike of the Celtic deities were always female.

Cuchulainn's travel to the isle of Scathach is particularly magical; it is an Otherworld journey undertaken by the hero to gain wisdom, skill, and most important of all, to be transformed. Cuchulainn left behind his two closest friends, Laegaire Battle Winner and Conall the Victorious; they lost heart and returned to Ulster.

First he crossed the Plain of Ill Luck; here the feet of men could stick fast and be pierced by razor-sharp grass blades; he entered the Perilous Glens filled with devouring beasts; then he came to the Bridge of the Cliff. This bridge tilted upwards whenever anyone tried to cross, throwing all comers to their death. Three times Cuchulainn tried to cross this bridge, which would give him access to the stronghold of Scathach, and three times he failed to cross. Finally, his heroic fervour came upon him, causing his face to shine like the sun (who was his father). Taking a great leap – the salmon leap – of the hero which involves twisting and turning against the flow – Cuchulainn landed in the middle of the tilting bridge. As it rose up vertically, he slid down to the other side.

At last he gained access to the stronghold of Scathach, and threatened her with his sword until she agreed to teach him all her famous skill in arms. Like so many hero sagas, this tuition, part of a bargain or test (for the hand of Emer) involved Cuchulainn in yet another task, for he fought and conquered Aoife, another warrior Queen as part of his bargain with Scathach. The curious wooing and winning of Emer is a primal version of a myth known all over Europe, rooted in pagan religious belief, in which a young power or hero must win the beautiful maiden from her ogre-like father or guardian.

Cuchulainn Marries Emer

When the newly skilled Cuchulainn returned to Ireland, he attacked the stronghold of Forgal the Wily in his scythed chariot. The fortress had triple walls, typical of the threefold symbolism of the Otherworld which repeatedly occurs in the tales about Cuchulainn.

Cuchulainn slew the defenders of the stronghold and finally killed Forgal. Pursued by the remaining warriors, whom he killed whenever they drew too close, Cuchulainn reached Emain Macha. There, after such a violent courtship and meeting, he married Emer. This remarkable couple, the ultimate hero and the most beautiful and skilled maiden in Ireland, were given honour and precedence in the court of King Conchobar MacNessa.

It seems unlikely that much of the above tale of Cuchulainn's wooing and marriage is based upon historical truth, yet there are many aspects to it which seem to be borne out by early Celtic tradition, custom, and evidence from literature and archaeology.

Once again we encounter a mixture of genuine cultural material; the tradition of warrior women, with idealised figures of the hero and his lover, fused into a myth of good overcoming evil, or perfection overcoming chaos.

Driven by Laeg, 'king of charioteers', the youthful Cuchulainn rides to battle and makes a chariot charge upon the hosts of Ireland. Such use of chariots and other weapons suggests that the Cuchulainn sagas come from an early Celtic heroic culture.

The Cattle Raid of Cooley

The most famous and extensive of the adventures of Cuchulainn is the tale of the war fought over the Brown Bull of Cualgne (pronounced 'Cooley').

The legend tells of two bulls of fairy or immortal lineage that were in Ireland at that time. When we use the word fairy in this context, we are not dealing with the weak tinsel creatures found in Victorian fantasies, but with the true fairies of Celtic tradition. These are powerful, terrible and beautiful immortal beings, similar to gods and goddesses, who are tall and fair to look upon. As late as the eighteenth and nineteenth century in Ireland and Scotland, Gaelic speakers still confirmed their belief in the people of the *sidhe* or fairy mound, and could still see them with the 'second sight'. The story goes on to say how the bulls were each transformed from other shapes and origins. First they were the swineherds of the gods Bodb (King of the Sidhe of Munster) and Ochne (King of the Sidhe of Connaught).

The two swineherds were in rivalry with one another, changing shape in pursuit of their endless quarrel. They became ravens to battle for a year, then water creatures, then they fought as human champions, and finally changed into eels. One of these magical eels swam into the River Cruind in Cualgne in Ulster, and was swallowed by a cow belonging to Daire of Cualgne. The other swam into the spring of Uaran Garad, in Connaught, where it was swallowed by a cow belonging to Queen Medb.

From this curious origin were born two bulls, the Brown Bull of Ulster, and the White Horned Bull of Connaught.

The Dispute

The White Bull was proud and scornful; he did not want to be the property of a woman, so he left the herds of Queen Medb and went into those of her husband Ailill. When the King and Queen counted their possessions one day, having nothing better to do, they found that they were equal in all things but one. Queen Medb had no bull to equal the White Bull in the herd of her husband Ailill.

So Medb sent bards with flattering gifts and words of praise to Daire, asking him to lend her the Brown Bull for the space of one year. Daire was about to agree to this request, when he overheard one of the Queen's men boasting that if the Bull was not lent freely, then the Queen would command her champions to take it by force. Naturally, Daire swore that under no circumstances would Queen Medb have the great Brown Bull.

So did the great war of the Cattle Raid begin; Queen Medb of Connaught raised all the armies of Ireland to fight against Ulster on account of the refusal of the loan of the Brown Bull. She made Fergus Mac Roich, an Ulster warrior who had previously quarrelled with King Conchobar MacNessa, the leader of this great host.

It was assumed that the war would be easy; the heroes of Ulster were suffering a magical sickness which came upon them each year as a result of an

The head was a sacred object to all the early Celts. This three-headed urn dates from the third century B.C. and is now in the Landesmuseum, Klagenfurt, Austria.

The boy hero killed the huge hound of Culann with his hurley stick, thus earning his name Cuchulainn, which means 'Hound of Culann'.

ancient curse laid upon them by a goddess who had once been insulted by an ancestor of King Conchobar. Queen Medb called up a prophetess and asked her what she saw of the warriors of Ulster. The account which follows is from a translation of the saga, edited by E. Hull, and the spelling of Irish names is thus not standardised:

So that night they pitched and encamped, and between the four fords of Aei – Athmaga, Athbercna, Athslisen, and Athcoltna – there was a mass of smoke and fire. Until the far end of a fortnight they tarried in Rath-Cruachan of Connacht, with quaffing and all pleasure, so that all the more lightly anon they should face their travel and their hosting. At which time it was that Meave bade her charioteer to put-to her horses for her; to the end she should go and confer with her wizard, to require of him foreknowledge and prophecy.

When she had gained the place where her magician was, she required of him foreknowledge and prediction accordingly, saying: 'Many there be which this day, and here, do part from their familiars and their friends, from their country and from their lands, from father and from mother. Now if so it be that not all of them return safe and sound, upon me it is that they will discharge their lamentation and their curses. For all which, however, there neither goes forth, nor yet stays there behind, any that to us is dearer than are we ourselves. Thou therefore find out for us whether we come back or not. The wizard answered: 'Whosoever comes or comes not, thou thyself shalt come.'

The driver wheels round the chariot, and the queen returns. But lo, she saw a thing that was a marvel to her: a woman close to her, on the chariot's shaft and facing her. The damsel's manner was this: in her right hand she held a weaver's sword of white bronze with seven beadings of red gold on its ends, and wove a bordering. A spot-pied cloak of green enveloped her, and in it at her breast there was a bulging massive brooch. She had a high-coloured, rich-blooded face; a blue and laughing eye; lips red and thin; glistening pearly teeth, which indeed you might have taken for a shower of white pearls fallen and packed into her head. Like unto fresh coral were her lips. Sweeter than strings of peaked harps played by long-practised masters' hands was the sweet sound of her voice, of her gentle utterance. Whiter than snow shed during a single night was the lustre of her skin and flesh, filtered through and past her raiment. Feet she had that were long and most white; nails pink and even, arched and pointed; fair-yellow gold-glittering hair: three tresses of it wound round her head, while yet another fell downwards and cast its shade below her knee.

Meave scanned her, and she said, 'Girl, at this time, and here, what doest thou?'

The young woman answered: 'I reveal thy chances and thy fortunes, and Ireland's four great provinces I gather up and muster against the Raid for the Kine of Cuailgne.'

18

'And for me wherefore dost thou this?'

'Great cause I have,' the girl explained; 'for I am a woman bondmaid of thy people.'

'And who art thou of my people?'

'I am Feidelm the prophetess, out of Cruachan's fairy hill.'

'Well, then, O prophetess Feidelm, how seest thou our host?'

'I see them all in red, I see them all becrimsoned.'

'Yet in Emania, Conachar for sure lies in his pangs,' said Meave; 'my messengers have been to him, and nought there is which we need fear from Ulster. But, Feidelm, tell us the truth of the matter: O woman-prophet Feidelm, how seest thou our host?'

'I see all red on them, I see crimson.'

'But Cuscraidh Menn Macha, Conachar's son, is in Iniscuscraidh in his pains; my messengers have been to him, and nought there is which we need dread from Ulster. But, Feidelm, tell us the truth of it: O Feidelm, O prophetess, how seest thou our host?'

'I see red on them, I see crimson.'

'But at Rathairthir, Eoghan mac Durthacht is in his pains: my messengers have been to him; nought is there which we need fear from Ulster. But, Feidelm, tell us true: Feidelm, thou woman-seer, how seest thou our host?'

'I see all red on them, I see all crimson.'

'Why, Celtchar mac Uitechar within his fort lies in his pangs: my messengers have been to him; nought is there which we need to fear from Ulster. But, O Feidelm, tell us true; woman-seer Feidelm, how seest thou our host?'

'I see red on them, I see crimson.'

'The manner in which thou deducest all this I approve not,' said Meave. 'For when the men of Erin shall have congregated to one place, among them doubtless will be quarrels and affrays and broils and onslaughts: as regards either taking the lead or bringing up the rear, concerning precedence at ford or river, concerning priority in killing a swine, a cow, a stag, or other game. But, Feidelm, tell me true: O prophetess Feidelm, how seest thou our host?'

'I see red on them, I see crimson. I see a small man who shall demonstrate weapon-feats,' . . . and here now she began to foretell and to foreshow Cuchulainn to the men of Erin, and she made a lay:

A small man I see, one who shall demonstrate weapon-feats, but at the price of many wounds in his smooth skin; the 'hero's light' is on his brow, and victory's arena his forehead is. The seven gems of an heroic champion are in the midst of both his eyes; his understanding is plain to perceive, and a red mantle, clasped, wraps him round. A face he has that is the noblest, best, and towards a woman-bevy great modesty he does observe; a stripling young and of complexion beautiful, but to the battle he shows a dragon's form. Like to Cuchulainn of Muirthemne his semblance and his valour are; who this Cú of Culann's from Muirthemne may be, I indeed know not, but this much full well I know: that by him the present host will all be red. In either one of both his hands, four small swords belonging to superlative sleight-feats he holds; he will attain to ply them on the host, an extraordinary act which drives men to eschew him. When, over and above his sword and spear, his *gae bulga* as

The sword was an important weapon of the Celts. This bronze hilt is from the second century B.C. and was found at North Grimston in Yorshire, England.

19

well he brings into play – he, the man who clad in scarlet mantle acts the sentinel – on all spaces he puts down his foot. His two spears point over the chariot's left; the frenzied one lets himself go: as to the form which to me hitherto has been revealed as worn by him, to me 'tis certain that his fashion he will change. For the battle now he sets forth, who unless he be provided against will prove to be a bane; for the combat 'tis he comes towards you, even Sualtach's son Cuchulainn. Your hosts now safe he will hew down, and make your slain to thickly lie: by him ye shall lose all your heads – she-prophet Feidelm conceals it not. From skins of heroes blood will pour, the memory of which shall be lasting, long; there shall be mangled bodies, women shall lamentation make, all by the 'Hound of the Forge,' whom now I see.

Thus far then the prediction and prognostication and the head and front of the story; with the occasion of its being found and made, and with the bolster-conversation which Ailell and Meave held in Cruachan.' (*The Cuchullin Saga* edited: E. Hall)

Cuchulainn was the only man in Ulster not affected by the curse of weakness; it was his task to defend almost single handed the Ulstermen against the hosts of Queen Medb.

Although Fergus had been insulted by King Conchobar, he sent a message warning the warriors of Ulster that the host of Medb was about to march upon them. Thus, Cuchulainn was keeping watch, forewarned, when the opposing army arrived.

Single Combat

Although an army set out to do battle, combat was primarily undertaken on a single basis; chosen warriors fought one another rather than an all-out pitched or mobile battle between all concerned. We find similar single combats in ancient poems such as the *Iliad* where the Greek warriors attacking Troy undertook selected duels to the death in order to settle specific aspects of the war. Equally, such single combat was seen as preferable to debilitating, all-out combat which would render both sides useless regardless of whoever gained the ultimate victory.

This economy of manpower is perhaps the basis of the ancient heroic single combat, for such fighting comes from times and cultures where manpower was scarce. Furthermore, it was regarded as the height of barbarism to waste many lives when allotted and specifically chosen champions were an integral part of the culture. It was the primary role of such champions to act for many men; this was their reason for living, fighting, and dying. In this sense, we might say that heroic warfare was more civilised than modern warfare in which thousands of lives are heedlessly wasted. The ancient concept of heroic combat persisted until as late as the Great War of 1914–18, in which early aerial combat retained some of this chivalric or heroic duelling quality. Paradoxically, this was also the war in which the modern concept of wasting many lives for the sake of relatively unimportant objectives was so strong a feature.

So we find the champion Cuchulainn as the sole defender of Ulster, while his companions are stricken by a magical weakness and sleep. Instead of merely overwhelming him by strength of numbers, as we might expect, the army of Queen Medb engages the hero in single combats, one after the other.

None of the warriors who challenged Cuchulainn returned; he killed them one by one. Between duels, he harassed the great army with his sling, slaying many men each day. He also killed the totem beasts belonging to the Queen; the dog, the bird, the squirrel. He generated such fear that no one dared to leave the camp. When one of the Queen's serving women wore her mistress's golden headdress, she was immediately slain by a well aimed stone from Cuchulainn's sling.

Eventually, Queen Medb, wanting to see this astonishing champion of Ulster face to face, sent a bard to ask Cuchulainn to parley. He agreed, and at the meeting Medb was amazed at his youth and seeming innocence. There he was, a mere seventeen years old, without a beard, yet destroying her vast army day after day. In the time honoured manner of powerful women, she offered the hero her own love and friendship, with great honour and possessions, if only he would come over to the side of Connaught and forsake Ulster. Despite his refusals, she repeated her offer over and over, until Cuchulainn warned that any further messengers of temptation would be slain.

In the end, he offered curious terms of battle, which the Queen was forced to accept. He agreed to fight one of the heroes of Ireland every day, and as long as the combat ensued, the main army was allowed to march forwards to gain ground. But as soon as the combat was over, the army must cease to move. Medb thought this a better bargain than to lose many men daily and gain no ground at all.

As an incentive to her warriors, Medb offered the love of her daughter Findabair (or Finnavar) who eventually died of maidenly shame on discovering that she had been the object of such a bargain. Yet despite the hand of the Queen's daughter as an incentive to do great deeds, not one hero of the army could kill Cuchulainn. However they did distract him sufficiently and Medb's men managed to steal the Brown Bull and fifty heifers while the hero was engaged in the series of combats.

The Morrigan

As with all ancient sagas or hero-cycles, the Cattle Raid of Cooley is a complex sequence combining myth and cultural history. After his remarkable exploits in single combat, reflecting actual styles of combat used by the ancient Celts, Cuchulainn next encountered a supernatural adversary.

So great were the warlike achievements of the Champion of Ulster that he attracted the attention of none other than the primal great goddess of war herself, known in Irish tradition as the Morrigan or Morrigu. It may be significant that in another legend altogether, Cuchulainn's grandfather, the Dagda, makes love to the Morrigan in an explicitly lusty creation and conflict myth. In other words, the Morrigu is concerned with the powers of life and death; as such she would be the natural patroness of heroes such as

Cuchulainn. While sleeping deeply and resting from his series of single combats, Cuchulainn was awakened by a great shout from the north, which in Celtic legend is the realm or region of the dead, justice and of the primal element of Earth. He ordered his driver Laeg to make the chariot ready and seek out the source of such a miraculous shout.

Travelling northwards, Cuchulainn met with a woman riding towards him in another chariot. She wore a red dress, a long red cloak, had red hair and eyebrows and carried a long grey spear. Courteous as all such heroes were, the Champion of Ulster hailed this apparition and asked her who she might be; she replied that she was a king's daughter who had fallen in love with him as a result of his wonderful exploits. This motif, in which a goddess seeks out a hero and declares her love for him is found in a number of myths world-wide, and has direct parallels in British and Greek tales from heroic cultures.

While Cuchulainn was adept at martial arts, he seems to have been rather naive when it came to recognising and dealing with supernatural beings, a failing common to many heroes. He told the red haired woman that he had more important things to concern himself with than a woman's love. The Morrigan then replied that she had been helping him throughout the battle, through her love for him, and that she would still continue to help him in return for his love. Unfortunately, Cuchulainn replied that he did not need any female help in battle. Despite the extremely broad clues as to her true identity, the Champion failed to recognise the goddess.

'If you will not have my love and help, then you shall have my hatred and enmity,' she said. 'When you are in combat with a warrior as good as yourself, I shall come against you in many shapes and hinder you, until your opponent has the advantage.'

Cuchulainn drew his sword to attack this threatening woman, but saw only a crow sitting upon a branch. The crow was the totem bird of the goddess, and then the Champion finally understood that he had rejected the help of the great goddess.

On the following day, a great warrior called Loch came to meet Cuchulainn in battle. Scornfully, he refused to fight a beardless youth, so Cuchulainn rubbed blackberry juice into his chin until it appeared darkened with a growing beard. Then the Champion discovered what it meant to have the goddess against him rather than for him; while he was in combat with Loch, she came against him three times. The first time she came in the shape of a heifer which tried to knock him over; the second time she came in the shape of an eel which wrapped around his legs as he stood in running water; the third time she came against him as a wolf that seized his sword arm.

But Cuchulainn broke the heifer's leg, trampled upon the eel, and poked out one of the eyes of the wolf. Yet every time he was hindered by these beasts, the warrior Loch wounded him deeply. Despite the worsening odds, Cuchulainn finally killed Loch with a cast of his magical spear, the thirty barbed *gae bulga* made from the bones of a sea monster.

After this threefold conflict and the hero's success against both goddess and champion, the Morrigan appeared again to Cuchulainn in the shape of an aged crone. She requested that he heal the wounds that he had inflicted upon her in her animal shapes, and finally a true pact was made between mortal and immortal.

Lugh and Cuchulainn

Just as the goddess appeared to Cuchulainn and ultimately helped him after conflict in which he was made fully aware that she was his patroness, so did his father the god Lugh appear. This sequence of apparitions and divine intervention is not merely a whim or trick of the story-teller's art; it is central both to the historical culture of the ancient Celts and to the magical, mythical and transformative adventures which the hero undertakes.

Cuchulainn's qualities are partly hereditary, from his parentage, and partly through training and support by the feminine personae of the warrior woman Scathach and the great goddess the Morrigan. Nevertheless, in some respects, he is still extremely young, and while showing natural strength and speed, trained skill, and remarkable qualities of endurance, he seems to be emotionally immature. Much of the hidden aspect of this sequence of tales leads the hero towards emotional and spiritual maturity. In this sense the hero sagas of the Celts are not dissimilar to the educational or exemplary tales connected to the martial arts in Eastern cultures; no matter how fast, strong or deadly the warrior is, it is ultimately his spiritual maturity that is at stake, not merely the winning and losing of battles.

Exhausted by continual combat, Cuchulainn suffered from lack of sleep; he could only snatch short rests, with his head on his hand, his hand on his spear, and his spear on his knee. Finally, his father Lugh the Long Handed took pity upon the champion, and appeared to him in the shape of a tall, handsome man in a green cloak, golden silk shirt covered with embroidery and carrying a black shield and five pointed spear. He cast his son into a magical sleep for three days and nights. While Cuchulainn slept, Lugh healed his many wounds with magical herbs; and when he awoke the Champion was completely refreshed and whole.

During this magical sleep, the boy troop of youthful warriors from Emain Macha came to fight against the army of Medb. Although they slew three times their own number, they were wiped out entirely.

Fergus and Cuchulainn

The next champion set against Cuchulainn in the war over the Brown Bull was his foster father Fergus. After much persuasion from Queen Medb, Fergus set out against the Champion, but without his famous sword. The two warriors made a remarkable agreement on the field of combat. For the sake of their years together when Cuchulainn was a child, Fergus asked Cuchulainn to only pretend to fight, and then to run away. Naturally, Cuchulainn declared that he was unwilling to be seen running away from

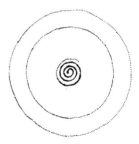

Impression of sharp-edged throwing shield as described in the Cuchulainn sagas.

anyone, even his own foster father. Fergus promised Cuchulainn that if he ran away on this occasion, then Fergus would, in turn, run away at some future time of Cuchulainn's choice. In this way, the Champion of Ulster showed some beginnings of wisdom, for he agreed to this trick, knowing that a future benefit might be superior to a momentary triumph, or even to the momentary shame of fleeing from combat. So during the man-to-man combat, Cuchulainn ran off and Fergus was able to return to the army and claim that he had fulfilled his duty.

Cuchulainn and Calatin

Next to be sent against the Champion of Ulster was the magician or Druid Calatin. Queen Medb ordered him to fight Cuchulainn with the assistance of his twenty seven sons and his grandson. This she justified by declaring that they were all of one body, that of Calatin, and that therefore she was not breaking the agreement to send only one man into combat.

The sons of Calatin had the notorious reputation of using poisoned spears which never missed their mark; any man wounded by such spears was soon certain to die. When Fergus heard of this dishonourable trick, he sent another Ulster exile called Fiacha to watch the combat and report back to him. Fiacha could not restrain himself from helping the outnumbered Cuchulainn, and between them the two warriors killed Calatin and his family.

Cuchulainn and Ferdiad

Medb now called upon the warrior Ferdiad who had been senior to Cuchulainn during the time of arms training on the island of Scathach. This provides an interesting insight into the manner in which such training schools were run, for Cuchulainn was Ferdiad's junior and servant during the early part of his training. Also the hero had been fostered to Fergus, a common practice among the Celtic tribes, leading to a stable structure of relationships between various families or clans. So another bond now appeared in the context of Ferdiad, who had a role similar to that of elder brother or senior student in arms.

At first Ferdiad refused to fight Cuchulainn, on account of their time together training under the instruction of Scathach. Queen Medb threatened that if he refused this combat, she would have him satirized so terribly that he would die of shame, and his name would be notorious for ever. This is a curious insight into the culture, for satire was not the weak concept of idle humour that it has become today. One thing that was feared by all champions, no matter how strong, was to be satirized by a poet. In a culture in which oral tradition held everything together (there being little or no written word) a satire would long outlast the memory of a living man. Satires were rapidly spread about the land, and any man who had been satirized was soon known to everyone as an object of insult and shame. Medb also offered a carrot with her stick, for she promised Ferdiad great rewards, and bound herself by a six-fold oath of surety that he would indeed be rewarded as promised.

So Ferdiad went reluctantly to combat. Cuchulainn met him with a warm welcome, but was told that his old companion had come to do battle rather than to celebrate friendship. They fought all day with neither gaining any advantage. At sunset, they retired to rest, and Cuchulainn sent half of his healing herbs to Ferdiad, while Ferdiad sent half of his food to Cuchulainn. Their horses were tended in the same stable, and their charioteers slept by the same fireside. This pattern was repeated on the second and third days, when they parted in great sorrow, knowing that on the next day one of them would die. This time the horses did not share a stall nor the charioteers share a fire; on the fourth day Cuchulainn killed his old companion with a low cast from his spear, the *gae bulga*.

When he saw Ferdiad dying, the battle frenzy faded from Cuchulainn. He took up the warrior into his arms, carrying him across the river so that he might die with the men of Ulster rather than with the army of Ireland as was the ancient custom. He made a lament over the body of Ferdiad, declaring that all had been a mere game and sport until this moment . . . 'yesterday Ferdiad was greater than a mountain, today he is less than a shadow.'

By this point in the conflict, the Champion of Ulster was so covered in wounds that he could not let his clothes touch his body, holding them off with hazel twigs and padding the spaces in between with moss and grass. The only part of his body not covered in wounds was the left hand which held his shield.

The Summoning of the Men of Ulster

Cuchulainn lay in this terribly wounded state, his groans of agony heard at great distance by his *human* father, Sualtam. The Champion persuaded his human father not to tend his wounds, but to ride immediately to the stronghold of Emain Macha and try to arouse the sleeping men of Ulster from their magical lethargy.

Bronze trumpet from Lough-na-Shade, Co. Armagh, Ireland.

Sualtam mounted upon Cuchulainn's great war horse Gray of Battle and made haste for the stronghold of King Conchobar. There, he gave three great shouts:

'Men are being killed, women stolen, and cattle lifted in Ulster!'

But no one heeded the first two shouts. With his third shout he partly awakened the Druid Cathbad, who cursed him for disturbing the sleep of the King.

So great was the rage of Sualtam, that he turned the horse sharply. As it reared, the sharp shield edge pressed against the rider's throat and cut off his head. The uncontrolled battle horse charged through the stronghold, with Sualtam's severed head still crying out:

'Men are being killed, women stolen, and cattle lifted in Ulster!'

Now the host truly awakened, and King Conchobar swore the most powerful oath known to the Celtic world, one which is found in a number of ancient tales, histories, and in oral tradition even today:

'The heavens are over us, the earth is beneath us, the seas encircle us; and unless the heavens with all their stars fall upon us or the earth gives way beneath us, or the seas flood in to drown the land, I will restore every cow to her stable and every woman to her rightful home!'

Messengers were sent to rally Ulster, and soon a battle was being fought such as had never before been seen in Ireland. Cuchulainn heard the noise of this great conflict, and despite his terrible wounds, arose to challenge Fergus as he led the army of Queen Medb. But rather than fight again, the Champion of Ulster reminded Fergus of his oath to run away when asked to do so; then Fergus ran from Cuchulainn, and when the great hosts saw their leader running, they ran also.

The Last Combat
The Brown Bull of Cualgne had travelled with the army into Connaught, where he challenged the White Bull of King Ailill. During the terrible battle which fell out between them, the Brown ripped the White to pieces, tossing his loins as far as Athlone and the liver to Trim. After this fight, the Brown Bull returned to Cualgne, where he became maddened with rage and killed all that moved before him. Finally, his heart burst with the power of his great bellowing, and so he died.

Thus ended the remarkable exploits of Cuchulainn during the Cattle Raid of Cooley.

Tragedy and Death

Like so many great heroic characters, the life of Cuchulainn is bound up not merely with stupendous feats of strength and martial skill, but also with unavoidable doom and tragedy. We found earlier how he had received his training in arms from the formidable warrior woman Scathach, and that during this training period he agreed to fight another warrior princess, Aoife, who he defeated and forced to bear him a son.

Cuchulainn Kills his Son
Cuchulainn's son Conlaoch (pronounced 'Connla') was the cause of tragedy through a subtle but inevitable process. When Aoife heard the news that Cuchulainn had married Emer, she decided to make the son into a weapon against his father. She taught him all her considerable skill in arms and sent him to Ireland; but before taking leave of her son, she put three *geasa* or immutable taboos upon him. The first was that he should not turn back, the second that he should never refuse a challenge, and the third was that he should never tell anyone his name.

When Conlaoch arrived at his father's home in Dundalk, he was met by the warrior Conall, who, according to most ancient custom asked him his name and lineage. Normally, he would have replied with his name, his father's name, and a list of his illustrious ancestors and relatives. This was an essential formality in the heroic culture of early Britain and Ireland; any man refusing to give such a lineage would have been highly suspect. Conlaoch's refusal, according to the *geas* laid upon him by his mother, caused Conall to challenge him to a duel, which of course Conall lost.

Next Cuchulainn himself came and asked the strange young man to reveal his lineage; Conlaoch replied:

'If I was not under a *geas* there would be no man in the world whom I would rather tell my lineage to, for I love your face.'

But the magical prohibitions of Aoife his mother had done their work, and father was forced to challenge son. In the terrible battle that followed, Cuchulainn shone with his famous hero light. Then Conlaoch realised that by a cruel twist of events he was fighting his own father, who he had come to find. He flung his spear sideways deliberately to miss the glowing hero, but Cuchulainn had already cast his terrible *gae bulga* which could not be withstood. The hero's son died, but not before he had identified himself to his father.

Cuchulainn's grief was terrible, and the men of Ulster were afraid that his madness would be turned violently upon them. In an attempt to save both the hero and his companions from further tragedy, the Druid Cathbad cast a spell upon Cuchulainn, such that he saw the waves of the sea as armed opponents. He battled with the waves until he collapsed from exhaustion.

The Final Battle

As might be expected in such a remarkable hero, Cuchulainn's death was brought about by a woman. Queen Medb, after her defeat in the Cattle Raid, held meetings with all the families who had had relatives killed by Cuchulainn. She worked upon them continually to seek revenge for their loved ones against the Champion of Ulster.

However, her deadliest weapons were the three daughters of Calatin the magician. She sent these three to Alba (Scotland) and to Babylon to learn magical arts.

When the three daughters returned from their training, they were able in every aspect of the magical arts, and could summon illusions of battle hosts with their formidable skills. Finally, Queen Medb waited until the period of weakness and lethargy fell upon the men of Ulster, just as she had done during the Cattle Raid. Thus, Cuchulainn faced alone her combined forces, both human and non-human.

As the massed forces of Queen Medb and her associates marched into Ulster and ravaged the land, King Conchobar MacNessa called a council of war. His warriors and Druids were too weak to fight, yet the King did not wish Cuchulainn to battle single-handed, for it was known that if the Champion fell, then the land would be luckless forever.

To keep the Champion from entering into battle until his fellow warriors were fit and active enough to assist him, the King ordered the women, the

An early Celtic bronze scabbard from Scotland, showing the grace and skill lavished upon their weapons by the early Celts of the Cuchulainn era.

bards, and the poets to divert Cuchulainn in every possible way, keeping him idle at Emain Macha. But while this desperate ploy was under way and Cuchulainn was feasting and talking, the three daughters of Calatin appeared. They created an illusory army out of grass, thistles and withered leaves, and caused the sound of trumpets and the roar and scream of battle to be heard all about Emain Macha.

Only when Cuchulainn was convinced by Conchobar's Druids that it was all an illusion did he restrain himself from rushing into battle. But it was clear to Conchobar that his Champion would soon be lured out into death unless he was further protected from enticements and tricks. The Champion was moved to the magical valley of Glean-na-Bodhar (Glen na Mower) which means 'Deaf Valley'; even if all the men in Ireland were to shout at once around this valley, no one inside would hear them.

Once again, the daughters of Calatin worked their arts of illusion, until it seemed that a vast host surrounded the valley, with fires raging and women shrieking. This noise reached even into the magical Deaf Valley, and although the women and Druids attending Cuchulainn tried to drown it, the Champion was certain that battle had come to his very resting place. Finally, Cathbad the Druid convinced Cuchulainn that it was still an illusion and that he need not venture out to battle.

But the last attempt to trick the champion into combat succeeded. One of the daughters of Calatin took the shape of a lover of Cuchulainn, crying out that Ulster was being ravaged. Despite all attempts to restrain him, Cuchulainn had his chariot harnessed and rode out to find the invading army. The omens for this last battle were bad; the Gray of Macha refused to be bridled and wept tears of blood; the Champion's mother Dechtire brought him wine three times, and each time it turned to blood when it touched his lips. When he crossed the first ford, he saw an Otherworld maiden washing clothes and armour, an important death vision. Just as if he was a stranger, or as if she did not recognise him in person, she told him that she washed the armour of Cuchulainn, who would shortly die.

Next the champion met three ancient hags roasting a hound on rowan spits. This apparition was an aspect of the Morrigan, the death goddess, and the hound was Cuchulainn's own totem animal as his name meant Hound of Culann. The three hags asked the Champion to share their feast, but it was taboo for him to eat the flesh of hound. Finally, they shamed him into eating, by saying that he was too proud to eat the humble food of three poor old women, yet was only too willing to spend his time idly feasting in the halls of chieftains and kings. It is significant that Cuchulainn failed to recognise what was happening, for he ate the meat, and by so doing half of his body was paralysed.

Cuchulainn carried three spears into battle, and each one, it was predicted, would kill a king. The first tactic used against the Champion of Ulster was that three Druids were sent to ask for the three spears; it was considered highly unlucky and dishonourable to refuse any request from a Druid.

When the Champion was in the midst of conflict, fighting the ravaging army single handed, the first Druid came up to him and asked him for his spear.

'Give me one of your spears, or I will satirize you . . .'

'Take it,' said the champion, 'Never have I been satirized for lack of generosity . . .' So saying he cast the spear at the Druid and killed him. But an opposing champion, Lugaid son of Curoi, took the spear and killed Laeg the charioteer. The loss of his charioteer was a desperate blow indeed, and with it the second Druid came to Cuchulainn and asked for a spear, saying that he would lampoon the province of Ulster if he was refused the gift.

'I need not give more than one gift in a day,' said Cuchulainn, 'But never let it be said that Ulster was satirized on my account . . .' and he threw the spear through the head of the Druid. But Erc the King of Leinster snatched the spear, and killed the Gray of Macha with it.

'Give me your spear,' asked the third and last Druid sent to Cuchulainn by his enemies, 'or I will satirize your kindred . . .' Once again, the champion speared the Druid, but this time Lugaid son of Curoi threw the spear back at Cuchulainn himself, wounding him to the death. Thus was the prophesy of the spears fulfilled, for Laeg had been king of the charioteers, and the Gray of Macha had been king of the horses, while Cuchulainn was the king of all champions.

In his death throes, Cuchulainn asked his enemies to allow him to reach a lake to drink and then return to the battle. He bound himself to a standing stone by the lakeside, so that he could fight and die standing up, for he had lost the ability to walk. Before its death, his horse, the Gray of Macha, supported him in battle, and killed fifty men with its teeth, and thirty with each of its hooves. But the hero light was fading from the Champion of Ulster and his face became as pale as snow. Finally, a crow, the death bird of the Morrigan, came and perched upon his shoulder.

A fine Celtic clasp showing a rider and two warriors fighting. If typifies both the attention to detail and the story telling elements frequently found in early Celtic culture and art across Europe.

Certain now that the Champion was dead, his enemies cut off his head.

With the death of Cuchulainn the power and prosperity of Emain Macha failed, as did the warriors of the Red Branch of Ulster.

Extracts from the Saga

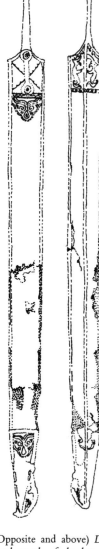

Having described the main adventures of Cuchulainn, and examined the primal heroic culture in which the warriors of Ulster lived, we can consider some examples from the early poems that preserve their legendary history.

The extracts which follow are taken from *The Cuchullin Saga* edited by Eleanor Hull in 1898, published by David Nutt of London. Spellings of Celtic language names were not standardised at this time, and the various translators who contributed used variant spellings, including the hero's name. The translations quoted have been selected to follow the main theme of our earlier chapters, and to demonstrate the rich colourful language and imagery of the sagas.

Firstly, we have a description of *The Hero*, which is both dramatic, powerful, and fantastic. Clearly, we are not being told of a human figure, but of a divine hero. Cuchulainn was the son of Lugh, the Sun God, and many of the features of our extract seem to indicate a magical image or god-form. The varying colours of his hair, multi-faceted eyes, and other attributes that seem bizarre to the modern reader are all associated with themes such as The Four Elements, the Seven Planets, and the mysterious powers of the Sun God. By way of contrast, we have a description of Ferdiad, Cuchulainn's heroic adversary; his appearance is more human, but clearly his arms and armour are of a magical and marvellous nature.

Our second example is a description of the famous *Battle Fury* of Cuchulainn. Once again, the imagery is full of magical potency, and terrible transformations. The historical Celts were noted by Greek and Roman historians for charging naked into battle, driven by a mystical frenzy that seemed to make them invincible; such behaviour persisted well into later centuries. Clansmen as late as the medieval period shunned armour, carried only small shields and the long Celtic sword, and even at that late period were still prone to charging naked into combat! The spirit of the Champion of Ulster was shared by many lesser heroes. In this quotation we also have a description of the armoured, spiked, and scythed chariot sometimes used by Cuchulainn.

The third extract is of a very different nature, being *Cuchulainn's Instructions to a Prince*. It is easy to forget, amidst the heroics and wonders, that the early Celts had a complex sophisticated culture. There were many rules of conduct rooted in an oral tradition of honour, religion, and tribal unity. The set of instructions reflect some of the concepts that underpinned Celtic culture for many centuries.

In *Cuchulainn and the Morrigan* we return to the supernatural theme that

(Opposite and above) Decorated swords of the late Iron Age, from the La Tene Celtic culture of around the fourth century B.C.

underpins his adventures. It is partly through his relationship to this primal Celtic goddess of death, procreation, and life, that Cuchulainn is so successful, for she is also goddess of war. Only after she withdraws her support can the Champion of Ulster be defeated.

Our last translation is *The Death of Cuchulainn* in which the desperate and in many ways ritualised end of the hero is described in detail.

The Hero

'A handsome lad truly was he that stood there; Cuchulainn son of Sualtam. Three colours of hair had he; next to the skin of his head the hair was brown; in the middle it was crimson; on the outside it was like a diadem of gold; comparable to yellow gold was each glittering long curling splendid beautiful thread of hair, falling freely down between his two shoulders.

About his neck were a hundred tiny links of red gold flashing, with pendants hung from them. His headgear was adorned with a hundred differ-

The modern, romantic statue of Cuchulainn which stands in Dublin Post Office, Eire.

ent jewels. On either cheek he had four moles, a yellow, a green, a blue and a red. In either eye he had seven pupils, sparkling like seven gems. Each of his feet had seven toes, each of his hands seven fingers; his hands and feet were endowed with the clutching power of hawk's talons and hedgehog's claws.

He wore his gorgeous raiment for great gatherings; a fair crimson tunic of five plies all fringed, with a long pin of white silver gold encased and patterned, shining like a luminous torch with a brilliance that men could not endure to look upon. Next to his skin was a body vestment of silk, bordered and fringed all around with gold, silver and white bronze braided together. His silken vestment came to the upper edge of his russet coloured kilt.

The champion carried a trusty special shield coloured dark crimson with a pure white silver rim all around its circumference; at his left side hung a long golden hilted sword. Beside him in his chariot was a lengthy spear, together with a keen aggressive javelin fitted with a hurling thong and rivets of white bronze. In one hand he carried nine heads, and nine more in the other; he held these heads as emblems of his valour and skill in arms, and at the sight of him the opposing army shook with terror.'

'And Ferdiad put on his battle suit of armour before the coming of Cuchulainn. It was a kilt of striped silk with a border of spangled gold next to his white skin. Outside, well sown over it was an apron of brown leather over the lower part of his body. Over that again he placed a stone as big as a millstone to defend his body below. And above all he put on his firm, deep apron of purified iron over the great stone, through dread of the *gae bulga* on that day.

Upon his head he wore his crested helmet of battle on which were four gems flashing in each quarter; it was studded all over with crystals and precious stones and *cruan* and with the brilliant rubies of the eastern world. In his right hand he took his destructive sharp pointed strong spear, and on his left side hung his curved sword of battle with a golden hilt and red pommel of gold. He slung upon his back his huge large bossed beautiful shield on which were fifty bosses each of which would bear the weight of a full grown hog, and with a great central boss of red gold.'

Cuchulainn in Battle Fury

'Then it was that he suffered his *riastradh* or paroxysm, whereby he became a fearsome and multiform and wondrous and hitherto unknown being. All over him, from his crown to the ground, his flesh and every limb and joint and point and articulation of him quivered as does a tree, yea a bulrush, in mid-current.

Within in his skin he put forth an unnatural effort of his body: his feet, his shins, and his knees shifted themselves and were behind him; his heels and calves and hams were displaced to the front of his leg-bones, in condition such that their knotted muscles stood up in lumps large as the clenched fist of a fighting man. The frontal sinews of his head were dragged to the back of his neck, where they showed in lumps bigger than the head of a man-child aged

While still a beardless boy, Cuchulainn slew three great champions and cut off their heads. Primal Celtic culture regarded the head as a sacred object of power, and head hunting was part of the ritual of war.

Three-headed deity, a recurrent theme, on a Celtic vase from Bavay, France. Cuchulainn himself is described as transforming his face during fits of frenzy, linking human and divine powers.

one month. Then his face underwent an extraordinary transformation: one eye became engulfed in his head so far that 'tis a question whether a wild heron could have got at it where it lay against his occiput, to drag it out upon the surface of his cheek; the other eye on the contrary protruded suddenly, and of itself so rested upon the cheek. His mouth was twisted awry till it met his ears. His lion's gnashings caused flakes of fire, each one larger than fleece of three-year-old wether, to stream from his throat into his mouth and so outwards. The sounding blows of the heart that panted within him were as the howl of a ban-dog doing his office, or of a lion in the act of charging bears.

Among the clouds over his head were visible the virulent pouring showers and sparks of ruddy fire which the seething of his savage wrath caused to mount up above him. His hair became tangled about his head, as it had been branches of a red thorn-bush stuffed into a strongly fenced gap to block it; over the which though a prime apple-tree had been shaken, yet may we surmise that never an apple of them would have reached the ground, but rather that all would have been held impaled each on an individual hair as it bristled on him for fury.

His hero's paroxysm projected itself out of his forehead, and showed longer than the whet-stone of a first-rate man-at-arms. Taller, thicker, more rigid, longer than mast of a great ship was the perpendicular jet of dusky blood which out of his scalp's very central point shot upwards and then was scattered to the four cardinal points; whereby was formed a magic mist of gloom resembling the smoky pall that drapes a regal dwelling, what time a king at night-fall of a winter's day draws near to it.'

The Battle Chariot

'This distortion being now past which had been operated in Cuchulainn, he leaped into the scythed chariot that was equipped with iron points, with thin edges, with hooks, with hard spit-spikes, with machinery for opening it, with sharp nails that studded over its axles and straps and curved parts and

The Morrigan – the terrifying Irish goddess of war, death, and procreation – confronts Cuchulainn. During his combats with the warriors of Queen Medb, Cuchulainn was first aided by the Morrigan; then through his own ignorance of her divinity, he caused her to turn against him.

Gold bracelet (La Tene style) typical of the type of adornments worn by Cuchulainn. This is from the Celtic region of Bad Durkheim, Germany. Celtic jewellery spread across Europe with movement of tribes and through trade.

tackle. Then he delivered a thunder-feat of a hundred, one of two hundred, one of three hundred, one of four hundred, and stood at a thunder-feat of five hundred; and he went so far, because he felt it to be obligatory on him that in this his first set-to and grappling with the four provinces of Erin, even such a number must fall by his hand. In which guise then he goes forward to assault his enemies, lending the chariot such impulse that its iron shod wheels sank in the earth and made ruts which well might have served as earth-works of defence; for both stones and rocks, both flags and the earth's bottom-gravel on either hand were heaped up outside the wheels and to an equal height with them.

The reason which moved him this day to make such hostile demonstration round about the men of Erin for he careered round them in a circle was that he designed thus to ensure that they should not escape him, neither should dissolve away from him, before he should have avenged the boy-corps on them. Then he charged them, and all round the host on their outer side he drew a fence built up of his enemies' carcasses. An onfall of a foeman on foemen indeed was this attack of his, for they fell sole to sole and trunk to trunk. Thrice in this wise he made the circuit of them, thereby leaving them laid in slaughter: the soles of three against the headless bodies of three more.'

Instructions from Cuchulainn to a Prince

The detailed instructions which follow – in their originally translated style – are a curious mixture of pagan Celtic ritual and belief, and of a code of conduct which is most familiar to the modern reader as that of King Arthur and the Knights of the Round Table. It is likely that the material was drawn from an enduring oral tradition, preserved by bards or poets, but elaborated and refined through repeated transcription and commentary by monastic chroniclers who finally set the Cuchulainn tales into written form:

34

'A meeting of the four great provinces of Erin was held at this time, to seek out a person on whom should be bestowed the sovereignty of Erin; because it was deemed an evil that the Hill of Supremacy and Lordship of Erin, Tara namely; should be without the rule of a king; moreover, they deemed it an evil that the tribes should be without a king's government to judge their houses. For a period of seven years the men of Erin had been without the government of a king over them; that is, from the death of Conaire at Bruidhen da Derga to the time of this great meeting of the four provinces of Erin in the court of Erc, son of Cairbre at Tara of the Kings.

Now these were the princes that were gathered to that meeting: Meave and Ailell, Curói, Tighernach son of Luchta, and Finn Mac Rossa. These would not admit the Ultonians to their council in the election of a king, because they were of one accord opposed to Ulster.

A bull-feast was prepared by them, that by its means they might discover on whom the sovereignty should be bestowed.

This was the manner in which the bull-feast was prepared. A white bull was killed, and one man ate his sufficiency of the flesh and of the broth; and he slept after having partaken of that meal, and a charm of truth was pronounced upon him by four druids. Then in a dream was shown to him the form of the man who should be made king, and his appearance and manner, with the sort of work that he was engaged in. Out of his sleep the man uttered a cry and he described to the kings the thing he saw, namely, a young man strong and noble, with two red streaks around him, and he sitting over the pillow of a man in a decline in Emain Macha.

Then was a message sent with this description to Emain Macha. Now the men of Ulster were at that time gathered round Conachar in Emania, where Cuchulainn lay upon his bed of sickness. The messenger told his story to the king and to the nobles of Ulster also. Then said Conachar, 'There is with us a free and nobly descended youth of that description, namely Lugaid, the son of

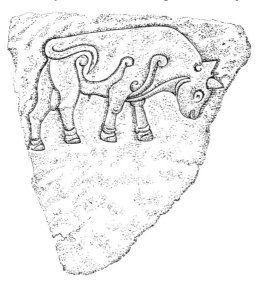

Typical Pictish/Celtic style bull, as shown in many carvings and manuscripts, and one of the great magical or sacred animals of the Celts.

35

Iron and bronze linchpin from a chariot wheel (La Tene style). The chariot was one of the principle weapons used by the early Celts, and features prominently in the Cuchulainn sagas.

the Three Fair Twins: the pupil of Cuchulainn; over whose pillow he sits alone within, solacing his tutor, that is Cuchulainn, who is in his bed of decline.

Suddenly Cuchulainn arose and began to instruct his pupil. These are his words:

"Stir not up sharp and ignoble contests. Be not flighty, inaccessible, haughty. Be not intractable, proud, precipitate, passionate. Be not bent down by the intoxication of much wealth.

Be not like a flea who fouls the ale in the house of a provincial king. Make not long sojourn on the frontiers of strangers. Do not visit obscure persons and those without power. Let not prescription close on illegal possession. Let witnesses be examined as to who is rightful heir of the land. Let the historians combine to act uprightly before you. Let the lands of the brethren, and their increase, be ascertained in their lifetime. Let the genealogical trees be added to as children are born. Let the living be called to their possessions; on the security of their oaths let the habitations of their ancestors be revived. Let the heir be established in his lawful patrimony. Let strangers be driven out by force of arms.

Speak not haughtily. Discourse not noisily. Mock not, insult not, deride not the old. Think not ill of any. Make no demands that cannot be met. [Grant nothing, refuse nothing, lend nothing without good cause.] Receive submissively the instructions of the wise. Be mindful of the admonitions of the old. Follow the decrees of your fathers.

Be not cold-hearted to friends, but against your foes be vigorous. Avoid dishonourable disputes in your many contests. Be not a tattler and abuser. Waste not, hoard not, alienate not. Submit to reproof for unbecoming deeds. Do not sacrifice justice to the passions of men. Lay not hands on the possessions of others, lest you repent it. Compete not, that you may not excite jealousy; be not lazy, lest you become weakened; be not importunate, lest you become contemptible. Do you consent to follow these counsels my son?"

Then Lugaid answered Cuchulainn in these words: "These precepts are worthy to observed without exception. All men shall see that none of them shall be neglected. They shall be executed if it be possible."

Lugaid then returned to Tara with the messengers. He was proclaimed King. That night he slept at Tara, after which all of the assembly returned to their own homes.'

(trans: *Book of the Dun Cow*)

Cuchulainn and the Morrigan

When Cuchulainn lay in sleep in Dún Imrid, he heard a cry sounding out of the north, a cry terrible and fearful to his ears. Out of a deep slumber he was aroused by it so suddenly, that he fell out of his bed upon the ground like a sack, in the east wing of the house.

He rushed forth without weapons, until he gained the open air, his wife following him with his armour and his garments. He perceived Laegh in his harnessed chariot coming towards him from Ferta Laig in the North. 'What brings thee here?' said Cuchulainn. 'A cry that I heard sounding across the plain,' said Laegh. 'From which direction?' said Cuchulainn. 'From the north-west,' said Laegh, 'across the great highway leading to Caill Cuan.' 'Let us follow the sound,' said Cuchulainn.

They go forward as far as Ath da Ferta. When they arrived there, they heard the rattle of a chariot from the loamy district of Culgaire. They saw before them a chariot harnessed with a chestnut horse. The horse had (but) one leg, and the pole of the chariot passed through its body, so that the peg in front met the halter passing across its forehead. Within the chariot sat a woman, her eye-brows red, and a crimson mantle round her. Her mantle fell behind her between the wheels of the chariot so that it swept along the ground. A big man went along beside the chariot. He also wore a coat of crimson, and on his back he carried a forked staff of hazelwood, while he drove a cow before him.

'The cow is not pleased to be driven on by you,' said Cuchulainn. 'She does not belong to you,' said the woman; 'the cow is not owned by any of your friends or associates.' 'The cows of Ulster belong to me,' said Cuchulainn. 'You would give a decision about the cow!' said the woman; 'you are taking too much upon yourself, O Cuchulainn!'

'Why is it the woman who accosts me?' said Cuchulainn. 'Why is it not the man?' 'It is not the man to whom you addressed yourself,' said the woman. 'Oh yes,' said Cuchulainn, 'but it is you who answer for him.' 'He is Uar-gaeth-sceo Luachair-sceo.' 'Well, to be sure, the length of the name is astonishing!' said Cuchulainn. 'Talk to me then yourself, for the man does not answer. What is your own name?' 'The woman to whom you speak,' said the man, 'is called Faebor beg-beoil cuimdiuir folt scenb-gairit sceo uath.'

'You are making a fool of me!' said Cuchulainn. And he made a leap into the chariot. He put his two feet on her two shoulders, and his spear on the parting of her hair.

'Do not play your sharp weapons on me!' she said. 'Then tell your true name,' said Cuchulainn. 'Go further off from me then,' said she. 'I am a female satirist, and he is Daire mac Fiachna of Cuailgne; I carry off this cow as a reward for a poem.' 'Let us hear your poem,' said Cuchulainn. 'Only move further off,' said the woman. 'Your shaking over my head will not influence me.' Then he moved off until he was between the two wheels of the chariot. Then she sang to him. . . .

Cuchulainn prepared to spring again into the chariot; but horse, woman, chariot, man, and cow, all had disappeared.

Then he perceived that she had been transformed into a black bird on a branch close by him. 'A dangerous enchanted woman you are!' said Cuchulainn. 'Henceforth this Grellach shall bear the name of the 'enchanted place'' (dolluid),' said the woman; and Grellach Dolluid was it called.

'If I had only known that it was you,' said Cuchulainn, 'we should not

The Sheela-na-gig *a primal goddess of sexuality, found in various carvings in Britain and Ireland. The savage Morrigan may be related to this type of image.*

37

have parted thus.' 'Whatever you have done,' said she, 'will bring you ill-luck.' 'You cannot harm me,' said he. 'Certainly I can,' said the woman. 'I am guarding your death-bed, and I shall be guarding it henceforth. I brought this cow out of the *Sídh* of Cruachan so that she might breed by the bull of Daire mac Fiachna, namely the Donn of Cuailgne. So long as her calf shall be a yearling, so long shall thy life be; and it is this that shall cause the Táin Bó Cuailgne.'

'My name shall be all the more renowned in consequence of this Táin,' said the hero:

> I shall strike down their warriors
> I shall fight their battles
> I shall survive the Táin!

'How wilt thou manage that?' said the woman; 'for, when thou art engaged in a combat with a man as strong, as victorious, as dexterous, as terrible, as untiring, as noble, as brave, as great as thyself, I will become an eel, and I will throw a noose round they feet in the ford, so that heavy odds will be against thee.'

'I swear by the God by whom the Ultonians swear,' said Cuchulainn, 'that I will bruise thee against a green stone of the ford; and thou never shalt have any remedy from me if thou leavest me not.' 'I shall also become a grey wolf for thee, and I will take from thy right hand, as far as to thy left arm.'

'I will encounter thee with my spear,' said he, 'until thy left or right eye is forced out; and thou shalt never have help from me, if thou leavest me not.'

'I will become a white red-eared cow,' said she, 'and I will go into the pond beside the ford, in which thou art in deadly combat with a man, as skilful in feats as thyself, and an hundred white red-eared cows behind me; and I and all behind me will rush into the ford, and the ''Faithfulness of men'' will be brought to a test that day, and thy head shall be cut off from thee.'

'I will with my sling make a cast against thee,' said he, 'so that thy right or thy left leg will be broken, and thou shalt never have help from me, if thou dost not leave me.'

Thereupon the Morrigu departed into the *Sídh* of Cruachan in Connacht, and Cuchulainn returned to his dwelling.

Cuchulainn's Death (from the *Book of Leinster*)

When Cuchulainn's foes came for the last time against him, the land was filled with smoke and flame; weapons fell from their racks, and the day of his death drew nigh.

The evil tidings were brought to him, and the maiden Levarcham bade him arise, though he was foreworn with fighting in defence of the plain of Muirthemne. Niamh, wife of Conall the Victorious, also urged him, so that he sprang to his arms, and flung his mantle about him; but the brooch fell and pierced his foot, forewarning him.

Then he took his shield, and ordered his charioteer, Laegh, to harness his horse, the Gray of Macha. But Laegh said: 'I swear by the God by whom my

The triple goddess on a Roman-Celtic carving from Cirencester, England. This persistent theme emphasises multiple head and eyes as Celtic symbols of divine power.

people swear, that though all the men of Conchobar's fifth were round the Gray of Macha, they could not bring him to the chariot. I never gainsaid thee until to-day. Come, then, if thou wilt, and speak with the Gray himself.'

Cuchulainn went to him. And thrice did the horse turn his left side to his master. On the night before, the Morrigu had unyoked the chariot, for she liked not Cuchulainn going to the battle, for she knew that he would not come again to Emain Macha.

Then Cuchulainn reproached his steed, saying that he was not wont to deal thus with his master. Thereat the Gray of Macha came, and let his big round tears of blood fall on Cuchulainn's feet. And Cuchulainn leaped into the chariot, and started southwards along the road of Mid-Luachair.

And Levarcham met him, and besought him not to leave them; and the thrice fifty queens who were in Emain Macha, and who loved him, cried to him with a great cry. But he turned his chariot to the right, and they gave a scream of wailing and lamentation, and smote their hands, for they knew that he could not come to them again.

The house of his nurse that had fostered him was on this road. He used to go to it whenever he went driving past from the north or south, and she kept for him always a vessel, with drink therein. He drank a drink and fared forth, bidding his nurse farewell. Then he saw somewhat, the Three Crones blind of the left eye, before him on the road.

They had cooked a hound with poisons and spells on spits of the rowan-tree. Now, one of the things that Cuchulainn was bound not to do, was to go to a cooking-hearth and consume the food. Another of the things that he must not do, was to eat his namesake's flesh. He speeds on, and was about to pass them, for he knew that they were not there for his good.

Then said the Crone to him, 'Stay with us a while, O Cuchulainn.'

'I will not stay with you, in sooth,' said Cuchulainn.

'That is because the food is only a hound,' quoth she. 'Were this a great cooking-hearth thou wouldst have visited us. But, because what is here is little, thou comest not. Unseemly is it for the great to despise the small.'

Then he drew nigh to her, and the Crone gave him the shoulder-blade of the hound out of her left hand. Then Cuchulainn ate it out of his (left) hand, and put it under his left thigh. The hand that took it, and the thigh under which he put it, were stricken from trunk to end, so that their former strength abode not in them.

Then he drove along the road of Mid-Luachair around Sliab Fuad; and his enemy, Erc son of Cairpre, saw him in his chariot, with his sword shining redly in his hand and the light of valour hovering over him, and his three-hued hair like strings of golden thread over an anvil's edge beneath some cunning craftsman's hand.

'That man is coming towards us, O men of Erin!' said Erc. 'Await him.' So they made a fence of their linked shields, and at each corner Erc made them place two of their bravest, feigning to fight each other, and a satirist with each of these pairs; and he told the satirists to ask Cuchulainn for his spear, for the sons of Calatin had prophesied of his spear that a king should be slain thereby unless it were given when demanded.

And he made the men of Erin utter a great cry, and Cuchulainn rushed against him in his chariot, performing his three thunder-feats; and he plied his spear and sword so that the halves of their heads and skulls and hands and feet, and their red bones were scattered broadcast throughout the plain of Muirthemne, in number like unto the sand of the sea, and the stars of heaven; like dewdrops in May, and flakes of snow and hailstones; like leaves of the forests and buttercups on Magh Breagh and grass under the feet of the herds on a summer's day. And grey was that field with their brains after the onslaught and plying of weapons which Cuchulainn dealt out to them.

Then he saw one of the pairs of warriors contending together, and the satirist called on him to intervene, and Cuchulainn leaped at them, and with two blows of his fist dashed out their brains.

'Thy spear to me!' says the satirist.

'I swear by the oath of my people,' said Cuchulainn, 'thou dost not need it more than I myself do. The men of Erin are upon me here, and I too am upon them.'

'I will revile thee if thou givest it not,' says the satirist.

'I have never yet been reviled because of my niggardliness or my churlishness,' said Cuchulainn, and with that he flung the spear at him with its handle foremost; and it passed through his head and killed nine on the other side of him. And Cuchulainn drove through the host, but Lugaid son of Curói got the spear.

'What will fall by this spear, O sons of Calatin?' said Lugaid.

'A king will fall by that spear,' say they.

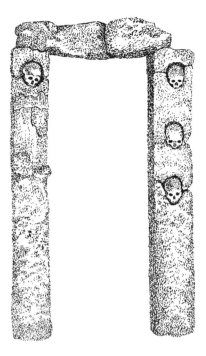

Then Lugaid flung the spear at Cuchulainn's chariot and it reached the charioteer, Laegh son of Riangabar, and all his bowels came forth on the cushion of the chariot.

'Then,' said Laegh, 'bitterly have I been wounded, etc.'

Thereupon Cuchulainn drew out the spear and Laegh bade him farewell. Then said Cuchulainn, 'Today I shall be champion and I shall also be charioteer.'

Then he saw the second pair contending, and one of them said it was a shame for him not to intervene. And Cuchulainn sprang upon them and dashed them into pieces against a rock.

'That spear to me, O Cuchulainn!' said the satirist.

'I swear by the oath of my people, thou dost not need the spear more than I do. On my head and my valour and my weapons it rests to-day to sweep the four provinces of Erin from the plain of Muirthemne.'

'I will revile thee,' says the satirist.

'I am not bound to grant more than one request in one day; and moreover, I have already saved my honour by payment.'

'Then I will revile Ulster for thy default,' says the satirist.

'Never yet hath Ulster been reviled on account of any refusal or churlishness of mine. Though little of my life remains to me, Ulster shall not be reviled this day.'

Then Cuchulainn cast the spear at him by the handle, and it went through his head and killed nine behind him, and Cuchulainn passed through the host even as we said before. But Erc son of Cairpre took the spear.

'What shall fall by this spear, O sons of Calatin?' says Erc, son of Cairpre.

Niches for sacred heads were a feature of Celtic sites, as in this reconstruction of the religious sanctuary at Roquepertuse, Bouches du Rhône, France.

41

'A king falls by that spear,' say the sons of Calatin.

'I heard you say that a king would fall by the spear which Lugaid long since cast,' he replied.

'And that is true,' say the sons of Calatin, 'thereby fell the King of the Charioteers of Erin, namely Cuchulainn's charioteeer, Laegh mac Riangabra.'

Thereupon Erc cast the spear at him and it lighted on the Gray of Macha. Cuchulainn snatched out the spear, and each of them bade the other farewell. Threat the Gray of Macha left him with half the yoke hanging from his neck, and went into Gray's Linn in Sliab Fuad. Then Cuchulainn drove through the host, and saw the third pair contending, and he intervened as he had done before. The satirist demanded his spear, and Cuchulainn at first refused it.

'I will revile thee,' quoth the satirist.

'I have paid for mine honour to-day. I am not bound to grant more than one request in one day.'

'Then I will revile Ulster for thy default.'

'I have paid for the honour of Ulster,' said Cuchulainn.

'I will then revile thy race,' said the satirist.

'Tidings that I have been defamed shall not go back to the land to which I myself shall never return; for little of my life remains to me,' said the hero. So Cuchulainn flung the spear to him, handle foremost, and it went through his head and through thrice nine other men.

' 'Tis grace with wrath, O Cuchulainn,' says the satirist.

Then Cuchulainn for the last time drove through the host, and Lugaid took the spear and said, 'What shall fall by this spear, O sons of Calatin?'

'A king will fall thereby,' say the sons of Calatin.

'I heard you say that a king would fall by the spear that Erc cast this morning.'

'That is true,' say they; 'the King of the Steeds of Erin fell by it, namely the Gray of Macha.'

Then Lugaid flung the spear and struck Cuchulainn, and his bowels came forth on the cushion of the chariot, and his only horse, the Black Sainglend, fled away, with half the yoke hanging to him, and left the chariot and his master, the King of the Heroes of Erin, dying alone upon the plain.

Then said Cuchulainn, 'I would fain go as far as that loch to drink a drink thereout.'

'We give thee leave,' said they; 'provided that thou come to us again.'

'I will bid you come for me,' said Cuchulainn, 'unless I shall return to you myself.'

Then he gathered his bowels into his breast, and went on to the loch. And he drank his drink, and washed himself, and came forth to die, calling on his foes to come and meet him.

Now a great mearing went westwards from the loch, and his eye lit upon it, and he went to the pillar-stone that is in the plain, and he put his

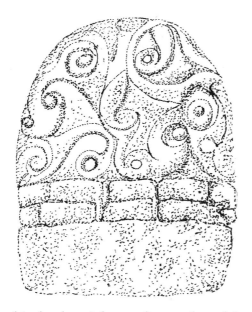

The Turoe Stone, a late Iron Age cult stone from Ireland.

breast-girdle round it that he might not die seated nor lying down, but that he might die standing up. Then came the men around him, but they durst not go to him, for they thought he was alive.

'It is a shame for you,' said Erc, son of Cairpre, 'not to take that man's head in revenge for my father's head that was taken by him.'

Then came to Cuchulainn the Gray of Macha to protect him, so long as his soul was in him, and the 'hero's light' out of his forehead shone above him. And the Gray of Macha wrought the three red onsets around him. And fifty fell by his teeth and thirty by each of his hoofs. Hence is the saying: 'Not keener were the victorious courses of the Gray of Macha after Cuchulainn's slaughter.'

Then came the birds and settled on his shoulder.

'There were not wont to be birds about that pillar,' said Erc, son of Cairpre. Then Lugaid arranged Cuchulainn's hair over his shoulder, and cut off his head. And the sword fell from Cuchulainn's hand, and it smote off Lugaid's right hand, so that it fell to the ground. And they struck off Cuchulainn's right hand in revenge for this. Then Lugaid and the hosts marched away, carrying with them Cuchulainn's head and his right hand, and they came to Tara, and there is the grave of his head and his right hand, and the full of the cover of the shield of mould.

From Tara they marched southward to the river Liffey. But meanwhile the hosts of Ulster were hurrying to attack their foes, and Conall the Victorious, driving forward in front of them, met the Gray of Macha streaming with blood. Then Conall knew that Cuchulainn had been slain. Together he and the Gray of Macha sought Cuchulainn's body. They saw the corpse of Cuchulainn at the pillar-stone. Then went the Gray of Macha and laid his head on Cuchulainn's breast. And Conall said, 'A heavy care is that corpse to the Gray of Macha.'

43

Then Conall followed the hosts, meditating vengeance, for he was bound to avenge Cuchulainn. For there was a comrade's covenant between Cuchulainn and Conall the Victorious, namely, that whichever of them was first killed should be avenged by the other.

'And if I be the first killed,' said Cuchulainn, 'how soon wilt thou avenge me?'

'On thy death-day,' said Conall, 'before its evening I will avenge thee. And if I be the first slain,' says Conall, 'how soon wilt thou avenge me?'

'They blood will not be cold upon the earth,' says Cuchulainn, 'before I shall avenge thee.'

So Conall pursued Lugaid to the Liffey.

There was Lugaid bathing. 'Keep a look-out over the plain,' he said to his charioteer, 'that no one come upon us without being seen.'

The charioteer looked past him.

'A single horseman is coming to us,' said he, 'and great are the speed and swiftness with which he comes.

Thou wouldst deem that all the ravens of Erin were above him. Thou wouldst deem that flakes of snow were specking the plain before him.'

'Unbeloved is the horseman that comes there,' says Lugaid. 'It is Conall the Victorious mounted on Dewy-Red. The birds thou sawest above him are the sods from the horse's hoofs. The snow-flakes thou sawest specking the plain before him are the foam from the horse's lips and from the bits of the bridle. Look again,' says Lugaid, 'by what road is he coming?'

'He is coming to the ford, the path that the hosts have taken,' answered the charioteer.

'Let that horse pass us,' said Lugaid; 'we desire not to fight against him.'

But when Conall reached the middle of the ford he spied Lugaid and his charioteer and went to them.

'Welcome is a debtor's face!' said Conall. 'He to whom thou owest debts demands them of thee. I am thy creditor,' continues Conall, 'for the slaying of my comrade Cuchulainn, and here I stand suing thee for it.'

Then it was agreed to fight on the plain of Argetros, and there Conall wounded Lugaid with his javelin. Thence they went to a place called Ferta Lugdach.

'I wish,' said Lugaid, 'to have men's truth from thee.'

'What is that?' said Conall the Victorious.

'That thou shouldst use only one hand against me, for one hand only have I.'

'Thou shalt have that,' says Conall the Victorious.

So Conall's hand was bound to his side with a cord. There, for the space between two watches of the day, they fought, and neither of them prevailed over the other.

When Conall found that he prevailed not, he saw his steed the Dewy-Red by Lugaid. And the steed came close to Lugaid and tore a piece out of his side.

'Woe is me!' said Lugaid, 'that is not men's truth, O Conall.'

'I gave it thee only on my own behalf,' said Conall; 'I gave it not on behalf of savage beasts and senseless things.'

'I know now,' said Lugaid, 'that thou wilt not go till thou takest my head with thee, since we took Cuchulainn's head from him. Take therefore my head in addition to thine own, and add my realm to thy realm, and my valour to thy valour. For I prefer that thou shouldst be the best hero in Erin.'

Then Conall the Victorious cut off Lugaid's head. And Conall and his Ulstermen returned to Emain Macha. That week they made no triumphal entry.

But the soul of Cuchulainn appeared there to the thrice fifty queens who had loved him, and they saw him floating in his spirit-chariot over Emain Macha, and they heard him chant a mystic song of the Coming of Christ and the Day of Doom.

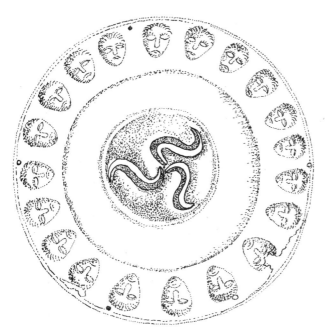

Early Celtic silver horse decoration, showing severed heads and the triskele or triple symbol of divinity.

45

Emain Macha

Emain Macha, now known as Navan Fort, is situated in Northern Ireland a few miles west of Armagh. It is the ancient royal capital of Ulster and is associated with Celtic culture, both through the Cuchulainn saga and from the evidence of archaeology. Its present condition is that of a large mound inside an immense circular hilltop enclosure. The term 'fort' is an unfortunate hangover from early days of archaeology, for like the royal enclosure of Tara in Meath (once seat of the High Kings of Ireland), Emain Macha is more likely to have been a ritual site rather than a defensive one. The site forms part of a complex in the area, which includes Lough na Shade nearby, where skulls, bones, and a remarkable bronze trumpet were found in the eighteenth century.

There is evidence of use from the Neolithic period, four to five thousand years ago, and occupation from around 600–100 B.C. It is this last period that is likely to connect to the tales of Cuchulainn, King Conchobar, and the warriors of Ulster, though some of the material preserved in the sagas could equally apply to much earlier Celtic culture. Excavation has shown that around 100 B.C., the site was considerably enlarged; a complex and sophisticated structure approximately 120 feet in diameter was built, consisting of five concentric circles of about 275 posts, with a large central post approximately 36 feet in height. With its original roof, this structure formed a huge conical building, very similar to those described in the sagas. Clearly, the poems preserved by later Christian monks echoed oral tradition and collective or family memory of this impressive period of development. The vast building is likely to have been a ritual centre for the people of the region.

Within a short period of its building, boulders were piled between the posts and the entire structure set alight. The remains were then covered with earth and turf, eventually creating the grassy mound which can still be seen today. Archaeologists suggest that this burning and mound-building was of religious rather than of military significance; destructive invaders would not be likely to commemorate their victory with such careful cairn building and covering of the remains.

Although some excavation was made as early as 1963, research was not completed until 1971, and has not yet been published. Certain famous artefacts have found their way to museums from earlier discoveries in the region.

Emain Macha, Navan Fort, associated with the warriors of Ulster in Irish tradition.

Character Names

This is a short list of names occuring in the narrative, with their role or function briefly described.

Aoife A warrior woman defeated by Cuchulainn
Brugh Na Boyne Prehistoric site; dwelling place of gods
Calatin Evil magician serving Queen Medb
Cathbad Druid serving King Conchobar
Conchobar King of Ulster
Conlaoch The son of Cuchulainn
Cuchulainn The Champion of Ulster
Dechtire Mother of Cuchulainn
Emain Macha Navan Fort, seat of King Conchobar
Emer Wife of Cuchulainn

Ferdiad Hero, brother in arms to Cuchulainn
Fergus Mac Roich Foster father of Cuchulainn
Fiacha An Ulster exile in Medb's army
gae bulga A thirty-barbed spear
Laeg Charioteer to Cuchulainn
Loch A champion of Queen Medb
Lugh The Sun God (father of Cuchulainn)
Medb Queen of Connaught
Morrigan or Morrigu Goddess of war, death, life, sexuality
Scathach Warrior woman who trains Cuchulainn
Setanta Original name of Cuchulainn
Sualtam Human father of Cuchulainn
Tain Bo Chuailnge The Cattle Raid of Cooley, the epic poem

Further Reading

Gantz, J. (trans.) *The Mabinogion* Penguin, Harmondsworth, 1976
Hull, E. *The Cuchulainn Saga* London, 1898
Kinsella, T. (trans.) *The Tain* London, 1970
McCana, P. *Celtic Mythology* London, 1970
Meyer, K. and Nutt, A. *The Voyage of Bran* London, 1898

Newark, T. *Celtic Warriors* Blandford Press, Poole, 1986
Rees, A. and B. *Celtic Heritage* London, 1961
Ross, A. *Pagan Celtic Britain* London, 1974
Stewart, B. and Matthews, J. *Warriors of Arthur* Blandford Press, London, 1987

Illustrations

Colour plates by James Field.
Line illustrations by Chesca Potter.
Map by Chartwell Illustrators.
Photographs courtesy of: British Museum (page 7); HMSO/Department of the Environment Northern Ireland (page 46); Irish Tourist Board (page 13); Peter Newark's Historical Pictures (pages 8 and 9); Scottish Tourist Board (page 15).

Index

Page numbers in *italics* refer to illustrations.